LETTERS ON THE CALCULATION OF EASTER

LETTERS ON THE CALCULATION OF EASTER

DIONYSIUS EXIGUUS

Copyright 2024 by Dalcassian Press

All rights reserved. No part of this book may be reproduced in any manner whatsoever without written permission except in the case of brief quotations embodied in critical articles and reviews.

No part of this publication may be reproduced, distributed, or transmitted in any form or by any means, including photocopying, recording, or other electronic or mechanical methods, without the prior written permission of the publisher, except in the case of brief quotations embodied in critical reviews and certain other non-commercial uses permitted by copyright law. For permission requests, write to Dalcassian Press at admin@thescriptoriumproject.com

Translator: Curtin, D.P. (1985-)

ISBN: 979-8-3482-6552-6 (Paperback)
ISBN: 979-8-3482-6553-3 (eBook)
Library of Congress Control Number:

Printed by Ingram Content Group, 1 Ingram Blvd, La Vergne, Tennessee
First Printing 2024, Dalcassian Press, Wilmington, DE

This work is part of a series produced in association with the Scriptorium Project and its community of scholars and translators.
Please visit our website at: www.thescriptoriumproject.com

1

Letter One

WRITTEN IN THE YEAR OF CHRIST, UNDER THE CONSULSHIP OF PROBUS, IN THE THIRD INDICTION.

To the most blessed and exceedingly desired Father Petronius, bishop, Dionysius Exiguus.

We have now endeavored to explain the calculation of the Paschal feast, which many have long frequently requested from us, aided by your prayers: following in all things the absolute and true sentence of the venerable three hundred and eighteen bishops who convened in the city of Nicaea in Bithynia against the madness of Arius, who established the observance of the fourteenth days of the Paschal feast as stable and unmovable, always fixing them in the returning cycle of nineteen years: which flow through all ages from the same beginning without the lapse of variety. However, this rule of the aforementioned cycle was sanctioned not so much by singular expertise as by the illumination of the Holy Spirit, and it is seen as having firmly and steadfastly appended an anchor to this reasoning of lunar measurement: which afterwards some, either despising through arrogance or transgressing through ignorance, induced by Jewish fables, delivered a different and contrary form of the unique feast. And because no structure can stand without the solidity of a foundation, they preferred to set the Lord's Pascha and the computation of the moon in some years in a far different manner, arranging disordered cycles: which not only lack any stability of return but also present a notable error in their course.

But the blessed Athanasius, archbishop of the city of Alexandria, who himself was then a deacon of the holy bishop Alexander at the Council of Nicaea, and who was present as an assistant in all things; and afterwards the venerable Theophilus and Cyril, did not deviate in the least from this venerable constitution of the synod. Rather, they diligently retained the same nineteen-year cycle, which is called Enneacaidecaeteris in Greek, and they are shown to have interspersed the Paschal course with no diversities. Finally, Pope Theophilus, dedicating a hundred-year cycle to the senior prince Theodosius, and the holy Cyril composing a cycle of ninety-five years, have preserved this tradition of the holy council for observing the fourteenth days of the Paschal feast in all respects. And because for those who are studious and seeking to know what is true, the rule of the same cycle ought to adhere more firmly, we believed this to be worthy of being inscribed after our preface. We have striven to elucidate this cycle of ninety-five years as best we could: presenting the last of the blessed Cyril, that is, the fifth cycle, since six years still remained from it, in this our work: and thereafter we profess to have arranged five others according to the norm of the same pontiff, or rather of the aforementioned Council of Nicaea.

Since, however, the holy Cyril began the first cycle from the one hundred and fifty-third year of Diocletian and concluded the last in the two hundred and forty-seventh; we, beginning from the two hundred and forty-eighth year of the same tyrant rather than of a prince, did not wish to attach the memory of the impious and persecutor to our cycles; but rather chose to note the years from the Incarnation of our Lord Jesus Christ: so that the beginning of our hope might be more known to us, and the cause of human redemption, that is, the passion of our Redeemer, might shine more clearly.

Furthermore, we thought it necessary to admonish the reader that this cycle of ninety-five years which we have made, when the time has finished and begins to return to the same, does not in all respects maintain the proposed firmness. For although the years of our Lord Jesus Christ preserve their order in a continuous series, and the indictions run through the usual revolution of fifteen years, you will find the epacts, which the Greeks call, that is, the annual lunar additions of eleven, which return to themselves in the end of thirty days, noted with fixed rules, and you will also find the nineteen-year cycle and the same fourteenth days of Pascha discovered by the revolution of all ages: yet the similar tenor of constancy cannot be maintained by the concurrent days of the week and the days of the Lord's Pascha, nor the very day of the Lord. However, the computation of the concurrent weeks, which arises from the course of the sun, is terminated by a seven-year constant circuit. In this, you will take care to number one each year; in that only year in which it has been a bissextile, you will add two; which also causes this cycle of ninety-five years not to appear to be concordant with its recurrence in all respects. For while it does not dissent in other years, in those only in which a bissextile intervenes, the Lord's Pascha with its moon occurs in various ways of reasoning. But those who pass through all times by a fixed order can direct their stable circuit of movable cases without any difficulty. And therefore, after the completion of ninety-five years, when someone wishes to return diligently to the beginning of these things, let him not hasten to the fifth cycle of the holy Cyril, which we have necessarily proposed to ourselves, but let him watchfully run to our first; and in the order we have mentioned, let him support the progress of those who seem to stagger by those who retain a firm course.

We have also deemed it necessary to note with no less care that we should not be deceived in the recognition of the first month. For from this, nearly all the error of the paschal discrepancy arises, while the beginning of time is unknown. For when the Almighty Lord indicated to the children of Israel, who were being freed from Egyptian slavery, that this most sacred solemnity was to be celebrated, He said in the Book of Exodus to Moses and Aaron in the land of Egypt: "This month shall be the beginning of months; it shall be the first month of the year" (Exod. XII, 2). Likewise, it is stated there: "In the first month, on the fourteenth day of the month at evening, you shall eat unleavened bread until the twenty-first day of the month at evening" (Ibid., 18). In Deuteronomy, the same legislator Moses admonishes the people about this matter, saying: "Observe the month of new fruits, and the first of the spring season, that you may keep the Passover to the Lord your God, for in this month the Lord your God brought you out of Egypt by night" (Deuter. XVI, 1 et seq.). By such divine authority, it is clear that the paschal feast must be celebrated on the fourteenth day at evening of the first month, until the twenty-first. But because it is not clearly read where this month takes its beginning or where it ends, the aforementioned three hundred and eighteen pontiffs, diligently investigating the observance of ancient custom, and handed down from the holy Moses, as is reported in the seventh book of Ecclesiastical History, said that the beginning of the first month is to be made from the new moon occurring from the eighth of the Ides of March until the day of the Nones of April, and from the twelfth day of the Kalends of April until the fourteenth of the Kalends of May, the fourteenth moon is to be diligently sought. Since this does not revolve equally with the course of the sun, it follows that the occurrence of the vernal equinox is reached within such a span of days: which is specially noted from the twelfth day of the Kalends of April, according to the opinions of all the Easterners, and especially the Egyptians, who are most knowledgeable about calculations. In which also, if the fourteenth moon should happen to fall on Saturday (which is evident to occur once in ninety-five years), the following day, Sunday, that is, the eleventh of the Kalends of April, the fifteenth moon, the celebration of Passover is firmly established by the same holy synod without ambiguity. In all these ways, it is admonished that before the twelfth of the Kalends of April, no one should inquire about the fourteenth moon of the paschal feast; which would be established not as the first month, but as the last.

But we have also deemed it necessary to mention that those who estimate the moon's course to complete its circle in thirty days are greatly mistaken, counting twelve lunar months in three hundred sixty days; to which they also add five days, which antiquity called intercalary, so that they seem to fulfill the solar year. When a diligent inquiry into the truth has shown that in two lunar cycles, it should be counted not sixty days, but fifty-nine. Thus, in the twelve lunar months, the total of three hundred fifty-four days is collected; to which the Egyptians add their annual epacts, that is, eleven days, so that finally the lunar measure may be equal to the solar ratio. This is proven to be most true and certain by the opinion of the aforementioned Fathers: who, according to this Egyptian calculation, transmitted the observance of the fourteenth moons of the paschal feast. But some, being ignorant of such subtlety, or rather of sanction, while seeking other arguments of calculation, depart from the path of truth. Hence it often happens that when the aforementioned Fathers place the fourteenth moon, these suspect it to be the fifteenth; and that which is the twenty-first, they declare to be the twenty-second. But for us, who have love and care for the Christian religion, it is altogether necessary not to deviate in any way; but it is most fitting to observe the paschal rule established by them with the most sincere observance.

As for how we strive for the authority of these Fathers in the Churches spread throughout the whole world, it is no labor to show: since according to the council held at Nicaea not long after, it deemed that the definition they had initially proposed regarding the calculation of Easter should in no way be violated. Finally, in the holy canons, under title seventy-nine, which is the first of the Antiochene council, it is expressed in these words: "All who dare to dissolve the definition of the holy and great council that was convened at Nicaea, in the presence of the most pious and venerable prince Constantine, regarding the salvific solemnity of Easter, we deem to be excommunicated and to be expelled from the Church; if, however, they persist in contentiousness against those things which have been rightly decreed." And indeed, these words are said about the laity. If, however, any of those who preside over the Church, whether a bishop, a presbyter, or a deacon, after this definition attempts to subvert the people and disturb the Churches, to gather separately and celebrate Easter with the Jews; the holy synod has declared this person to be already alien from the Church, as it has been a cause of corruption and disturbance not only for themselves but also for many. It not only removes such from ministry but also those who, after such condemnation, attempt to communicate, have been condemned, and are deprived of all external honor, which the holy rule and the priesthood of God has merited. Similar to these, the venerable Pope Leo, the prelate of the apostolic see, pronounces, saying: "Against the statutes of the holy fathers, which were established in the city of Nicaea many years ago by spiritual decrees, no one is permitted to dare anything: so that if anyone wishes to decree something different, he rather diminishes himself than corrupts those." If these are kept intact by all bishops, there will be peace and firm concord throughout all the Churches. And again: "In all ecclesiastical matters, we obey these laws, which the Holy Spirit instituted for the peaceful observance of all priests through three hundred and eighteen bishops: so that even if many more decide something different from those, whatever has been different from the aforementioned constitution should not be held in any reverence."

It is sufficiently indicated to all, as we believe, that from now on the most sacred Easter should not be celebrated otherwise than as established by the holy Fathers. But if anyone, perhaps with a stubborn mind, despises the testimonies of such great priests, he will also find briefly mentioned in ecclesiastical history; and by the relation of many bishops, especially the blessed Athanasius, of whom we mentioned above, he will recognize the same published. The same indeed is testified by the letter of Saint Proterius, bishop of the city of Alexandria, directly to Pope Leo regarding this same Easter question, which we perceived should be added to this work by transferring from Greek; and we have also included the arguments sought by the sagacity of the Egyptians; by which, if they happen to be unknown, the Easter titles can easily be found: that is, which year it is from the Incarnation of the Lord, and what the indiction is; which lunar cycle or nineteen-year cycle exists; and the other similar calculations are required. May your blessedness be deemed worthy to be kept by divine grace praying for us.

2

Letter Two

WRITTEN IN THE YEAR OF CHRIST'S COMMON ERA.

To the most venerable lords Boniface, the first notary, and Bono, the second notary, Dionysius Exiguus sends greetings.

I have been compelled to commend the rule of the Paschal observance, long having been reminded by the holy and venerable Bishop Petronius, believing that all subsequent opposition to diversity would be removed; especially since I had endeavored with all my might to insinuate the authority of the three hundred and eighteen holy bishops who convened at Nicaea: who in that venerable council regularly affixed the nineteen-year cycle, noting the fourteenth lunar phases of the Paschal observance immovably throughout all times of their revolution. But since your holiness, concerning the question of this matter, has now brought forth the writings of the venerable Bishop Paschasios from the archives of the Roman Church, who is known to have presided for the most blessed Pope Leo in the holy Council of Chalcedon, which evidently agrees with the holy Fathers, we have added it to this present work: so that we might rely also on the testimony of this man, who confirms the Paschal decrees with a manifest miracle of venerable pontiffs. As for the mention of common years and embolismic years in the writings themselves, and this reasoning, which is said to descend from the tradition of the Hebrews, is greatly sought after by those wishing to know whether it seems to harmonize with the paternal rule; we deemed it necessary to summarize this knowledge, so that it may not be proved to disagree in any way, constrained by brevity.

We therefore know that the same nineteen-year cycle revolves continuously through the octad and the hendecad. The number itself is explained as eight and eleven. The octad, which begins with the first nineteen-year cycle, which is the lunar seventeenth, is carried out in this manner: it has the first and second years as common, that is, lesser; the third year as an embolismic, that is, greater; the fourth and fifth years again as common; the sixth as embolismic; the seventh as common, the eighth as embolismic. Thus, the octad has five common years and three embolisms continuously assigned. The common year collects twelve lunar months, which make three hundred fifty-four days. The embolismic year, however, is shown to have thirteen moons and three hundred eighty-four days. Similarly, the hendecad runs according to this law. It begins in the ninth year of the nineteen-year cycle, which is the lunar sixth: its first and second years are common, the third is embolismic; the fourth and fifth are common, the sixth is embolismic; the seventh and eighth are common; the ninth is embolismic; the tenth is common, the eleventh is embolismic: thus, the hendecad ends with seven common years and four embolisms. The rationale for the embolisms is proven to exist because it seems to compensate for the losses of the common years: insofar as the lunar excursion is equated to the solar time. For although the lunar circle surrounds the solar year through each month, it does not prevail in completing its perfection with twelve of its months. Ultimately, in common years, eleven lunar days are seen to be lacking in relation to the solar year. In embolisms, however, it seems that the lunar year transcends the solar by nineteen days. Therefore, let us bring forth the years of the octad and hendecad according to the order of the aforementioned cycle; and we will clearly prove that, through eight years and eleven, the course of the moon contends with the sun: when it collects as many days as the latter has run.

In the octad, we said there are five common years and three embolisms. Therefore, five times three hundred fifty-four becomes one thousand seven hundred seventy; and three times three hundred eighty-four becomes one thousand one hundred fifty-two, and thus together they amount to two thousand nine hundred twenty-two. Similarly, eight solar years, if reduced to a sum, that is, eight times three hundred sixty-five and a quarter, together make two thousand nine hundred twenty-two. In the same way, if you add the years of the hendecad, which are seven common and four embolismic, in the sum we have mentioned, you will find nearly the same amount as eleven solar years make, that is, four thousand fourteen. This is therefore the rationale of the embolisms, as we have said, to compensate for the losses of the common years with their increments.

But now I will show you the most beautiful and distinguished collection of the nineteen-year cycle, through which you may remove any ambiguity that may have arisen henceforth; nor should anyone be so struck by excessive wonder that he does not rejoice at the light of truth shown to him, and, leaving behind the darkness of ignorance, does not immediately acquiesce to such reasoning. From the fifteenth moon of the Paschal feast of the preceding year, for example, until the fourteenth of the following year, what we seek, if it is a common year, will have three hundred fifty-four days; if it is an embolismic year, three hundred eighty-four. If one day more or less occurs, it is an evident error. Except for the first year of the aforementioned nineteen-year cycle, which we wish to count from the fourteenth moon of the last Paschal feast, that is, the nineteenth year, until the fourteenth of the same first year. Therefore, the same last year retains eighty lunar epacts, that is, lunar additions, accommodating twelve days in the first year, not eleven, as is usually done in other years. And because they revolve at the end of thirty days, no epact is placed at the beginning of that cycle; however, the second year receives eleven epacts: and therefore, as we have said, from the fifteenth moon of the first cycle until its end, it is not doubtful that we find the fixed days in common and embolismic years. If at any time the incompetence of calculators has perhaps presented this differently, the falsehood of their reasoning will be argued by this observance.

And in order for this to be understood more clearly, let us demonstrate with the example of the present year. The fourth indiction is at hand, and the eleventh lunar circle; the nineteenth cycle is the fourteenth. And since it is the sixth year of the eleventh cycle, it must be an embolismic year. Therefore, let us diligently inquire how many days there are from the fifteenth moon of the past feast until the fourteenth of the present; and we shall undoubtedly find when we ought to celebrate Pascha. After the year has passed through the third indiction, on the fourteenth moon of Pascha, on the ninth day of the month of April, that is, the twenty-fourth day of March, who doubts, who has any care for this matter, however little they may know? And therefore, let us take the eighth day of the month of April as the starting point for our counting; we have seven days of March, thirty of April, thirty-one of May, thirty of June, thirty-one of July, thirty-one of August, thirty of September, thirty-one of October, thirty of November, thirty-one of December, thirty-one of January, twenty-eight of February, thirty-one of March, and twelve days of April, which is the day before the ides of April. In total, this makes three hundred eighty-four. But if, according to the definition of those who count the moon differently from the truth, we give the fourteenth not to the day before the ides of April, but to the third day before the ides; we shall collect three hundred eighty-three days with a reduced number; which is by no means permitted. And so, whenever such a doubt arises, let us carefully compute the days from the fifteenth moon of the past feast to the fourteenth of Pascha, which we seek. And if it is a common year, there are three hundred fifty-four days; if it is an embolismic year, we shall find three hundred eighty-four: nor will any inequality occur: because the rule of this cycle stands in this way, the detailed formula of which we present in the following description.

In the nineteenth year, the seventeenth lunar year, from the fifteenth day of the month of May to the ninth of April, since it is a common year, there are three hundred fifty-four days.

In the nineteenth year, the eighteenth lunar year, from the eighth day of the ides of April to the eighth day of the month of April, since it is common, there are three hundred fifty-four days.

In the nineteenth year, the nineteenth lunar year, from the seventh day of the month of April to the ides of April, since it is an embolismic year, there are three hundred eighty-four days.

In the nineteenth year, the first lunar year, from the eighteenth day of the month of May to the fourth day of the nones of April, since it is common, there are three hundred fifty-four days.

In the nineteenth year, the second lunar year, from the third day of the nones of April to the eleventh day of the month of April, since it is common, there are three hundred fifty-four days.

In the nineteenth year, the third lunar year, from the tenth day of the month of April to the fourth day of the ides of April, since it is an embolismic year, there are three hundred eighty-four days.

In the nineteenth year, the fourth lunar year, from the third day of the ides of April to the third day of the month of April, since it is common, there are three hundred fifty-four days.

In the nineteenth year, the fifth lunar year, from the day before the month of April to the fourteenth day of the month of May, since it is an embolismic year, there are three hundred eighty-four days.

In the nineteenth year, the sixth lunar year, from the thirteenth day of the month of May to the seventh day of the ides of April, since it is common, there are three hundred fifty-four days.

In the nineteenth year, the seventh lunar year, from the sixth day of the ides of April to the sixth day of the month of April, since it is common, there are three hundred fifty-four days.

In the nineteenth year, the eighth lunar year, from the fifth day of the month of May to the seventeenth day of the month of May, since it is an embolismic year, there are three hundred eighty-four days.

In the nineteenth year, the ninth lunar year, from the sixteenth day of the month of May to the day before the nones of April, since it is common, there are three hundred fifty-four days.

In the nineteenth year, the tenth lunar year, from the nones of April to the ninth day of the month of April, since it is common, there are three hundred fifty-four days.

In the nineteenth year, the eleventh lunar year, from the eighth day of the month of April to the second day of the ides of April, since it is an embolismic year, there are three hundred eighty-four days.

In the nineteenth year, the twelfth lunar year, from the ides of April to the month of April, since it is common, there are three hundred fifty-four days.

In the nineteenth year, the thirteenth lunar year, from the fourth day of the nones of April to the twelfth day of the month of April, since it is common, there are three hundred fifty-four days.

In the nineteenth year, the fourteenth lunar year, from the eighth day of the month of April to the second day of the ides of April, since it is an embolismic year, there are three hundred eighty-four days.

In the nineteenth year, the fifteenth lunar year, from the ides of April to the month of April, since it is common, there are three hundred fifty-four days.

In the nineteenth year, the sixteenth lunar year, from the fourth day of the nones of April to the twelfth day of the month of April, since it is common, there are three hundred fifty-four days.

In the nineteenth year, the seventeenth lunar year, from the eleventh day of the month of April to the fifth day of the ides of April, since it is an embolismic year, there are three hundred eighty-four days.

In the nineteenth year, the eighteenth lunar year, from the fourth day of the ides of April to the fourth day of the month of April, since it is common, there are three hundred fifty-four days.

In the nineteenth year, the nineteenth lunar year, from the third day of the month of April to the fifteenth day of the month of May, since it is an embolismic year, there are three hundred eighty-four days.

3

Latin Text

EPISTOLA I.
SCRIPTA ANNO CHRISTI, PROBO CONSULE, INDICTIONE 3.

Domino beatissimo, et nimium desideratissimo Patri Petronio episcopo, Dionysius Exiguus.

Paschalis festi rationem, quam multorum diu frequenter a nobis exposcit instantia, nunc adjuti precibus vestris explicare curavimus: sequentes per omnia venerabilium trecentorum et octodecim pontificum, qui apud Nicaeam civitatem Bithyniae contra vesaniam Arii convenerunt, etiam rei hujus absolutam veramque sententiam: qui quartasdecimas lunas paschalis observantiae per novemdecim annorum redeuntem semper in se circulum stabiles immotasque fixerunt: quae cunctis saeculis eodem quo repetuntur exordio sine varietatis labuntur excursu. Hanc autem regulam praefati circuli non tam peritia singulari quam sancti Spiritus illustratione sanxerunt, et velut anchoram firmam et stabilem huic rationi lunaris dimensionis apposuisse cernuntur: quam postmodum nonnulli vel arrogantia despicientes, vel transgredientes inscientia, Judaicis inducti fabulis, diversam atque contrariam formam festivitatis unicae tradiderunt. Et quia sine fundamenti soliditate non potest structura ulla consistere, longe aliter in quibusdam annis dominicum Pascha et lunae computum praefigere maluerunt, inordinatos circulos ordinantes: qui non solum nullam recursus stabilitatem, verum etiam cursum praeferunt errore notabilem.

Sed Alexandrinae urbis archiepiscopus beatus Athanasius, qui etiam ipse Nicaeno concilio tunc sancti Alexandri pontificis diaconus, et in omnibus adjutor interfuit; et deinceps venerabilis Theophilus, et Cyrillus, ab hac synodi veneranda constitutione minime desciverunt. Imo potius eumdem decemnovennalem circulum, qui Enneacaidecaeterida Graeco vocabulo nuncupatur, sollicite retinentes, paschalem cursum nullis diversitatibus interpolasse monstrantur. Papa denique Theophilus centum annorum cursum Theodosio seniori principi dedicans, et sanctus Cyrillus cyclum temporum nonaginta et quinque annorum componens, hanc sancti concilii traditionem ad observandas quartasdecimas lunas paschales per omnia servaverunt. Et quia studiosis, et quaerentibus scire quod verum est, debet ejusdem circuli regula fixius inhaerere, hanc post praefationem nostram credidimus ascribendam. Nonaginta quinque autem annorum hunc cyclum studio quo valuimus expedire contendimus: ultimum ejusdem beati Cyrilli, id est quintum circulum, quia sex adhuc ex eo anni supererant, in nostro hoc opere praeferentes: ac deinde quinque alios juxta normam ejusdem pontificis, imo potius saepe dicti Nicaeni concilii, nos ordinasse profitemur.

Quia vero sanctus Cyrillus primum cyclum ab anno Diocletiani centesimo quinquagesimo tertio coepit, et ultimum in ducentesimo quadragesimo septimo terminavit; nos a ducentesimo quadragesimo octavo anno ejusdem tyranni potius quam principis inchoantes, noluimus circulis nostris memoriam impii et persecutoris innectere; sed magis elegimus ab Incarnatione Domini nostri Jesu Christi annorum tempora praenotare: quatenus exordium spei nostrae notius nobis existeret, et causa reparationis humanae, id est passio Redemptoris nostri, evidentius eluceret.

Hoc praeterea lectorem putavimus admonendum, quod circulus iste nonaginta et quinque annorum quem fecimus, cum finito tempore in idipsum reverti coeperit, non per omnia propositam teneat firmitatem. Nam licet anni Domini nostri Jesu Christi ordinem suum continuata serie custodiant, et indictiones per annos quindecim solita revolutione decurrant, epactas etiam, quas Graeci vocant, id est adjectiones annuas lunares undecim, quae triginta dierum fine in se redeunt, fixis regulis invenias adnotatas, decemnovennalem quoque recursum, et paschales quartasdecimas lunas easdem omnium aevorum revolutione reperias: tamen tenorem similem constantiae nequeunt custodire concurrentes dies hebdomadum, et dies Paschae Domini, luraque ipsius diei Dominici. Concurrentium autem hebdomadum ratio, quae de solis cursu provenit, septeno annorum jugi circuitu terminatur. In quo per annos singulos unum numerare curabis; in eo tantummodo anno in quo bissextus fuerit, duos adjicies; quae causa etiam facit ut non per omnia circulus iste nonaginta quinque annorum suo recursui concordari videatur. Nam cum in caeteris annis non dissentiat, in illis solis in quibus se bissextus interserit, Pascha dominicum cum sua luna vario modo rationis occurrit. Sed hi qui ordine fixo per omnia decurrunt tempora, mobilium casuum sua stabili circuitione sine ulla possunt difficultate dirigere. Et ideo post expletionem nonaginta quinque annorum, cum harum rerum diligens ad exordium redire voluerit, non ad quintum cyclum sancti Cyrilli, quem nobis necessario proposuimus, sed ad nostrum primum vigilanter excurrat; et ordine, quo diximus, per eos qui firmum cursum retinent, eorum progressum, qui videntur titubare, sustentet.

Illud quoque non minori cura notandum esse censuimus, ne in primi mensis agnitione fallamur. Hinc enim pene cunctus error discrepantiae paschalis exoritur, dum temporis initium ignoratur. Nam cum Dominus omnipotens hanc sacratissimam solemnitatem celebrandam filiis Israel, qui ex Aegyptia servitute liberabantur, indiceret, ait in libro Exodi ad Moysen et Aaron in terra Aegypti: Mensis iste principium mensium, primus erit in mensibus anni (Exod. XII, 2).

Itemque ibidem: Primo, inquit, mense, decimo quarto die mensis ad vesperum comedetis azyma, usque ad vigesimum primum ejusdem ad vesperum (Ibid., 18). In Deuteronomio quoque idem legislator Moyses ita populum de hac re commonet dicens: Observa mensem noverum frugum, et verni primum temporis, ut facias Pascha Domino Deo tuo, quoniam in isto mense eduxit te Dominus Deus tuus de Aegypto noctu (Deuter. XVI, 1 et seq.). Tanta hac auctoritate divina claruit, primo mense, decimo quarto die ad vesperum, usque ad vigesimum primum, festivitatem paschalem debere celebrari. Sed quia mensis hic unde sumat exordium, vel ubi terminetur, evidenter ibi non legitur, praefati trecenti et octodecim pontifices, antiqui moris observantiam, et exinde a sancto Moyse traditam, sicut in septimo libro Ecclesiasticae refertur Historiae, solertius investigantes, ab octavo idus Martii, usque in diem nonarum Aprilium, natam lunam facere dixerunt primi mensis exordium: et a duodecimo die calendarum Aprilium usque in decimum quartum calendas Maias lunam decimam quartam solertius inquirendam. Quae quia cum solis cursu non aequaliter volvitur, tantorum dierum spatiis occursum vernalis aequinoctii consequatur: qui a duodecimo calendarum Aprilium die, cunctorum Orientalium sententiis, et maxime Aegyptiorum, qui calculationis prae omnibus gnari sunt, specialiter adnotatur. In quo etiam, si luna decima quarta sabbato contigerit (quod semel in nonaginta quinque annis accidere manifestum est), sequenti die dominico, id est undecimo calendas Aprilis, luna decima quinta, celebrandum Pascha, eadem sancta synodus sine ambiguitate firmavit. Hoc modis omnibus admonens, ut ante duodecimum calendas Aprilis lunam decimam quartam paschalis festi nullus inquireret; quam non primi mensis, sed ultimi esse constaret.

Sed nec hoc praetereundum esse putavimus, quod nimis errant qui lunam peragere cursum sui circuli triginta dierum spatiis aestimantes, duodecim lunares menses in trecentis sexaginta diebus annumerant; quibus etiam quinque dies adjiciunt, quos intercalares appellavit antiquitas, ut solarem annum adimplere videantur. Cum diligens inquisitio veritatis ostenderit in duobus lunae circulis non sexaginta dies, sed quinquaginta novem debere numerari. Ac per hoc in duodecim lunaribus mensibus trecentorum quinquaginta quatuor dierum summam colligi; cui epactas Aegyptii annuas, id est undecim dies, accommodant: ut ita demum lunaris emensio rationi solis adaequetur. Quod verissimum esse atque certissimum suprascriptorum Patrum sententia comprobatur: qui, juxta hanc Aegyptiorum calculationem, quartas decimas lunas paschalis observantiae tradiderunt. Sed nonnulli tantae subtilitatis, sive potius sanctionis ignari, dum alia supputationis argumenta perquirunt, a veritatis tramite recedunt. Unde plerumque contingit, ut quando saepe dicti Patres decimam quartam lunam ponunt, eam isti decimam quintam suspicentur; et quae vigesima prima est, vigesimam secundam esse pronuntient. Sed nobis, quibus amor et cura est Christianae religionis, nulla prorsus oportet ratione discedere; sed praefixam ab his paschalem regulam sincerissima convenit observatione servare.

Quanta vero in Ecclesiis toto terrarum orbe diffusis horum Patrum nitamur auctoritate, non labor est ostendere: cum secundum concilium apud Nicaeam post tempora non longa conveniens, eorum primitus definitionem, quam de paschali ratione protulerant, nullo modo violandam esse censuerit. Denique in sanctis canonibus, sub titulo septuagesimo nono, qui est primus ipsius Antiocheni concilii, his verbis invenitur expressum: Omnes qui ausi fuerint dissolvere definitionem sancti et magni concilii quod apud Nicaeam congregatum est, sub praesentia piissimi et venerandi principis Constantini, de salutifera solemnitate paschali, excommunicandos, et de Ecclesia pellendos esse censemus; si tamen contentiosi, adversus ea quae bene sunt decreta, perstiterint. Et haec quidem de laicis dicta sint. Si quis autem eorum qui praesunt Ecclesiae, aut episcopus, aut presbyter, aut diaconus, post hanc definitionem tentaverit ad subversionem populorum, et Ecclesiarum perturbationem, seorsim colligere, et cum Judaeis Pascha celebrare; sancta synodus hunc alienum jam hinc ab Ecclesia indicavit, quod non solum sibi, sed plurimis causa corruptionis ac perturbationis exstiterit. Nec solum a ministerio tales removet, sed etiam illi qui post damnationem hujusmodi communicare tentaverint, damnati sunt, omni quoque extrinsecus honore privati, quem sancta regula, et sacerdotium Dei promeruit. His non dissimilia venerabilis papa Leo sedis apostolicae praesul pronuntiat, dicens: Contra statuta canonum paternorum, quae ante longissimae aetatis annos in urbe Nicaea spiritalibus sunt fundata decretis, nihil cuiquam audere conceditur: ita ut si quis diversum quid velit decernere, se potius minuat, quam illa corrumpat. Quae si, ut oportet, a cunctis pontificibus intemerata serventur, per universas Ecclesias pax erit, et firma concordia. Et iterum: In omnibus, inquit, ecclesiasticis causis, his legibus obsequimur, quas ad pacificam observantiam omnium sacerdotum per trecentos octodecim antistites Spiritus sanctus instituit: ita ut etiamsi multo plures aliud, quam illi statuere, decernant, in nulla reverentia sit habendum, quidquid fuerit a praedictorum constitutione diversum.

Sufficienter, ut putamus, cunctis indicitur, ne deinceps aliter quam a sanctis constitutum est Patribus, sacratissimum Pascha celebretur. Quod si testimonia tantorum sacerdotum forsitan quis obstinata mente despexerit, etiam in historia ecclesiastica paria breviter intimata reperiet; multorumque relatione pontificum, et maxime beati Athanasii, cujus supra meminimus, haec eadem vulgata cognoscet. Idipsum vero epistola sancti Proterii Alexandrinae urbis episcopi ad eumdem papam Leonem pro hac eadem paschali quaestione directa, testatur: quam ante hos annos transferentes e Graeco, huic operi adnectendam esse perspeximus: nec non et argumenta Aegyptiorum sagacitate quaesita subdidimus; quibus, si forsitan ignorentur, paschales tituli possint facile reperiri: id est, quotus sit annus ab Incarnatione Domini, et quota sit indictio; quotus etiam lunaris circulus, sive decemnovennalis existat; caeterique simili supputationis compendio requirantur. Orantem pro nobis beatitudinem vestram divina gratia custodire dignetur.

EPISTOLA II.

SCRIPTA ANNO CHRISTI VULGARI.

Dominis a me plurimum venerandis Bonifacio primicerio notariorum, et Bono secundicerio, Dionysius Exiguus salutem.

Observantiae paschalis regulam, diu sancto ac venerabili Petronio episcopo commonente, tandem stylo commendare compulsus, omnem deinceps diversitatis oppugnationem sublatam fore credideram; maxime quod sanctorum trecentorum octodecim antistitum qui apud Nicaeam convenerant, auctoritatem totis nisibus insinuare curaveram: qui in ipso concilio venerando decemnovennalem cyclum regulariter affigentes, quartas decimas lunas paschalis observantiae per omnia tempora legi suae revolutionis immobiles adnotaverunt. Sed quoniam sanctitas vestra, orta rei hujus quaestione, de archivo Romanae Ecclesiae Paschasini venerabilis episcopi scripta, quem constat pro persona beatissimi papae Leonis sancto Chalcedonensi praesedisse concilio, ad eumdem papam per idem tempus directa nunc protulit, quae sanctis Patribus evidenti ratione consentiunt, huic praesenti indidimus operi: ut hujus etiam viri testimonio niteremur, qui manifesto miraculo venerabilium pontificum paschalia decreta confirmat. Quod vero in scriptis ipsis communium annorum et embolismorum mentio facta est, et a nonnullis haec ratio, quae ex Hebraeorum, ut fertur, traditione descendit, magnopere quaeritur, scire volentibus, utrum huic paterna regula consonare videatur; necessarium duximus, et hanc notitiam, ne probetur in aliquo dissidere, coacta brevitate digerere.

Noverimus itaque, quia idem decemnovennalis cyclus per ogdoadem et hendecadem semper in se revolvitur. Octo namque et undecim ipse numerus explicatur. Ogdoas ergo, quae incipit a primo decemnovennali cyclo, qui est lunaris decimus septimus, hac ratione peragitur, ut annos primum et secundum, communes, id est minores habeat, tertium embolismum, id est majorem; annum quartum et quintum item communes, sextum embolismum; septimum communem, octavum embolismum. Ac per hoc ogdoadis communes anni quinque, et tres embolismi jugiter ascribuntur. Communis autem annus duodecim lunares menses colligit, qui dies trecentos quinquaginta quatuor efficiunt. Embolismus autem annus, et lunas tredecim, et dies trecentos octoginta quatuor habere monstratur. Item hendecas hac lege discurrit. Incipit nono anno cycli decemnovennalis, qui est lunaris sextus: cujus primus et secundus annus communis est, tertius embolismus; quartus et quintus communis, sextus embolismus; septimus et octavus communis; nonus embolismus; decimus communis, undecimus embolismus: sicque hendecas communibus annis septem, embolismis quatuor terminatur. Embolismorum autem ista ratio probatur existere, quia annorum communium videtur damna supplere: quatenus ad solare tempus lunaris exaequetur excursio. Quamvis enim anni solaris circulum per singulos menses luna circumeat, tamen ejus perfectionem duodecim suis mensibus implere non praevalet. Denique in annis communibus ad rationem solaris anni undecim dies lunae deesse cernuntur. In embolismis vero novemdecim diebus eumdem annum videtur solarem luna transcendere. Quapropter ogdoadis et hendecadis annos, juxta praefati circuli ordinem, in medium proferamus; et liquido probabimus, per octo annos et undecim, lunae cursum cum sole contendere: quando tot dies illa colligat quot ille cucurrerit.

In ogdoade diximus quinque annos esse communes, tres embolismos. Quinquies ergo trecenteni quinquageni quaterni, fiunt mille septingenti septuaginta; et ter trecenteni octogeni quaterni, mille centum quinquaginta duo, ac per hoc simul fiunt bis mille nongenti viginti duo. Similiter octo anni solares, si in summam redigantur, id est octies trecenti sexageni quini, et quadrans, faciunt simul bis mille nongentos viginti duos. Simili modo et hendecadis annos, qui sunt communes septem, et quatuor embolismi, si in summam ea qua diximus supputatione congesseris, tantumdem pene reperies, quantum undecim solares anni conficiunt; hoc est, quater mille quatuordecim. Haec est ergo embolismorum, sicut praediximus, ratio, ut incrementis suis communium annorum detrimenta compensent.

Sed jam pulcherrimam vobis atque praeclaram collectionem ipsius cycli decemnovennalis ostendam, per quam omnem deinceps ambiguitatem, si qua mota fuerit, auferatis; nec sit ita quis nimio stupore perculsus, qui demonstrata sibi veritatis luce non gaudeat, et ignorantiae relictis tenebris, tantae rationi protinus non acquiescat. A decima quinta luna paschalis festi, anni, verbi gratia, praecedentis, usque ad decimam quartam sequentis, quod quaerimus, si communis annus est, trecentos quinquaginta quatuor dies habebit; si embolismus, trecentos octoginta quatuor. Quod si dies unus plus minusve contigerit, evidens error est. Excepto videlicet anno primo saepe dicti decemnovennalis cycli, quem a decima quarta luna Paschae ultimi, id est noni decimi anni, usque ad decimam quartam ejusdem primi numerare curamus. Propter quod idem ultimus epactas, id est adjectiones lunares, octodenas tunc retinens, primo anno, non undecim, ut caeteris annis fieri solet, sed duodecim dies accommodat. Et quia triginta dierum fine volvuntur, nulla epacta in principio ipsius cycli ponitur; secundus autem annus epactas undecim suscipit: et ideo, sicut diximus, a decima quinta luna Paschae primi cycli usque ad finem ejus, in communibus et embolismis annis praefixos dies nos invenire, non dubium est. Quod si aliter aliquando calculantium imperitia fuerit fortassis expositum, hac observantia ratiocinationis eorum falsitas arguetur.

Atque ut hoc manifestius possit intelligi, praesentis anni monstremus exemplo. Indictio quippe quarta est, et lunaris circulus undecimus; decemnovennalis cyclus decimus quartus. Et quoniam hendecadis sextus annus est, eum embolismum esse necesse est. A decima quinta itaque luna praeteriti festi, usque ad decimam quartam praesentis, quot sunt dies diligentius inquiramus: et inveniemus procul dubio, quando Pascha celebrare debeamus. Transacto anno per indictionem tertiam in Pascha lunam decimam quartam nono calendarum Aprilium die, id est vigesimo quarto mensis Martii fuisse, quis dubitet, qui curam hujus rei habere quantulumcunque cognoscitur? Et ideo ab octavo calendarum Aprilium die numerandi sumamus exordium; habemus Martii dies septem, Aprilis triginta, Maii triginta et unum, Junii triginta, Julii triginta et unum, Augusti triginta et unum, Septembris triginta, Octobris triginta et unum, Novembris triginta,

Decembris triginta et unum, Januarii triginta et unum, Februarii viginti octo, Martii triginta et unum, Aprilis duodecim dies, quod est pridie idus Aprilis. Fiunt simul trecenti octoginta quatuor. Quod si, juxta eorum diffinitionem, qui lunam aliter quam se veritas habet computant, decimam quartam non pridie iduum Aprilium, sed tertio iduum demus occurrere; trecentos octoginta tres dies imminuto numero colligemus; quod nullo fieri pacto conceditur. Et ita semper quotiens dubitatio talis occurrerit, a decima quinta luna transactae festivitatis, usque in decimam quartam Paschae, quod quaerimus, dies sollicite computemus. Et si communis annus est, trecentos quinquaginta quatuor dies; si embolismus est, trecentos octoginta quatuor inveniemus: nec inaequalitas (alias, inaequaliter) prorsus eveniet: quia regula cycli hujus hac ratione subsistit, cujus enucleatam formulam subjecta descriptione pandemus.

Anno decemnovennali primo, lunari decimo septimo, a decimo quinto calendas Maii usque nonas Aprilis, quia communis annus est, sunt dies trecenti quinquaginta quatuor.

Anno decemnovennali secundo, lunari decimo octavo, ab octavo idus Aprilis usque in octavum calendas Aprilis, quia communis est, sunt dies trecenti quinquaginta quatuor.

Anno decemnovennali tertio, lunari decimo nono, a septimo calendas Aprilis usque in idus Aprilis, quia embolismus est, fiunt dies trecenti octoginta quatuor.

Anno decemnovennali quarto, lunari primo, a decimo octavo calendas Maii usque in quartum nonas Aprilis, quia communis est, fiunt dies trecenti quinquaginta quatuor.

Anno decemnovennali quinto, lunari secundo, a tertio nonas Aprilis usque in undecimum calendas Aprilis, quia communis est, fiunt dies trecenti quinquaginta quatuor.

Anno decemnovennali sexto, lunari tertio, a decimo calendas Aprilis usque in quartum idus Aprilis, quia embolismus est, fiunt dies trecenti octoginta quatuor.

Anno decemnovennali septimo, lunari quarto, a tertio idus Aprilis usque in tertium calendas Aprilis, quia communis est, fiunt dies trecenti quinquaginta quatuor.

Anno decemnovennali octavo, lunari quinto, a pridie calendas Aprilis usque in decimum quartum calendas Maii, quia embolismus est, fiunt dies trecenti octoginta quatuor.

Anno decemnovennali nono, lunari sexto, a decimo tertio calendas Maii usque in septimum idus Aprilis, quia communis est, fiunt dies trecenti quinquaginta quatuor.

Anno decemnovennali decimo, lunari septimo, a sexto idus Aprilis usque in sextum calendas Aprilis, quia communis est, fiunt dies trecenti quinquaginta quatuor.

Anno decemnovennali undecimo, lunari octavo, a quinto calendas Aprilis usque in decimum septimum calendas Maii, quia embolismus est, fiunt dies trecenti octoginta quatuor.

Anno decemnovennali duodecimo, lunari nono, a decimo sexto calendas Maii usque in pridie nonas Aprilis, quia communis est, fiunt dies trecenti quinquaginta quatuor.

Anno decemnovennali decimo tertio, lunari decimo, a nonis Aprilis usque in nonum calendas Aprilis, quia communis est, fiunt dies trecenti quinquaginta quatuor.

Anno decemnovennali decimo quarto, lunari undecimo, ab octavo calendas Aprilis usque in secundum idus Aprilis, quia embolismus est, fiunt dies trecenti octoginta quatuor.

Anno decemnovennali decimo quinto, lunari duodecimo, ab idibus Aprilis usque in calendas Aprilis, quia communis est, hunt dies trecenti quinquaginta quatuor.

Anno decemnovennali decimo sexto, lunari decimo tertio, a quarto nonas Aprilis usque in duodecimum calendas Aprilis, quia communis est, fiunt dies trecenti quinquaginta quatuor.

Anno decemnovennali decimo septimo, lunari decimo quarto, ab undecimo calendas Aprilis usque in quintum idus Aprilis, quia embolismus est, fiunt dies trecenti octoginta quatuor.

Anno decemnovennali decimo octavo, lunari decimo quinto, a quarto idus Aprilis usque in quartum calendas Aprilis, quia communis est, fiunt dies trecenti quinquaginta quatuor.

Anno decemnovennali decimo nono, lunari decimo sexto, a tertio calendas Aprilis usque in decimum quintum calendas Maii, quia embolismus est, fiunt dies trecenti octoginta quatuor.

This work was produced in association with:

www.ingramcontent.com/pod-product-compliance
Lightning Source LLC
LaVergne TN
LVHW061049070526
838201LV00074B/5238